ENCLAVE

by Tato Laviera

D1566631

Arte Público Press

Houston, Texas

1981

Arte Público Press
Revista Chicano-Riqueña
University of Houston
Central Campus
Houston, Texas 77004

ISBN 0-934770-11-5

Printed in the United States of America

Book Jacket Design by José G. González
Cover Art by Fernando Salicrup

TABLE OF CONTENTS

Feelings of One

Oro in Gold

Prendas

Keys to Tato Laviera

When Tato raps, he fingersnaps. His poems are *en clave*, songs in the key of the many people with whom Tato Laviera seeks to strike up a rhythm, grounded most of the time on *la bomba*, "para siempre!", the Afro-Puerto Rican-New York percussive base, but spanning outward to embrace an eye-scratching range of neighboring beats, from Africa, the Caribbean and Latin America to Black American idiom—a warm and close affinity—and reaching out, still *en clave*, to *los chicanos* (don't miss "¡Vaya, Carnal!") and to John Lennon mourners everywhere. The colonial enclave can and does bring forth *prendas*, a new universalism, a friendly, curious sympathy with other people and their diverse cultures, particularly those like Tato's own Puerto Rican people engaged in struggles for liberation and full self-expression. "Métele encima el jazz, el rock o fox trot inglesa,/la bomba se va debajo, ay virgen no hay quien la mueva."

The poems in *Enclave*, and in Tato's first book, *La Carreta Made a U-Turn*, are Puerto Rican in this full sense, laying down synchronic bridges, however preliminary, toward adjacent rhythms, and activating all the various strains of the native Puerto Rican oral tradition: Afro-Puerto Rican poetry (Luis Palés Matos) and music *(la bomba* and *la plena)*, Spanish declamatory rhetoric (Juan Boria and Jorge Brandon), the *danza* ("María borinquen"), the *canción jíbara;* from reminiscences of the indigenous, Taíno legacy to *salsa* and the Latin hustle. Puerto Ricans are sky people, "la gente del cielo," "fingering on clouds,/ climbing further and further,/to preserve taíno folklore." And Puerto Rico, well Puerto Rico is a little island, "100 by 35 by 1000/mountains multiplied by the square root/of many cultures breathing: ONE." *Pura bomba* at the base, *para siempre*, but always transfigured, once drum beats are joined by dancing feet, the conjunto of instruments and the singing voice and the drama of barrio life.

Tato is a *plenero:* the trunk of his songs and *cantos negros*, rising up from *bomba* roots, is the distinctively Puerto Rican tradition of *la plena*. The poetry pays programmatic allegiance to that form time and again, notably in "el sonero mayor" (for the revered Ismael Rivera) from *La Carreta Made a U-Turn* and in "rafa," that splendid "search through plena history" in honor of Rafael Cortijo. It is clear that for Tato, a Black Puerto Rican from Santurce, the prominence of *la plena* is not simply a matter of personal inclination. *La plena* provides the sturdiest pillar of Puerto Rican cultural history, being both the watershed of inherited oral expression in its array of styles and currents and the springboard for experimentation, in the Puerto Rican key, in many new directions.

Whatever its etymology, *plena* means full, and has come to be recognized—at least since Tomás Blanco's landmark essay "Elogio de 'la plena'" (1935)—as the genre of popular song specific to the Puerto Rican people, akin to other Caribbean forms and resting, of course, on African rhythmic footing, but developed as a tradition only in Puerto Rico. It is the full flowering of the national music, superceding the elite and imported *danza* and ushering the slave, peasant and working-class voice to the forefront of the country's unique field of creative expression: "as we detail contributions/so we must all stand/gracious ovation/rafael cortijo/unanimous consensus/puerto rican people." Tato is in his element, I would say, when delivering his own *plenas*—most of them already set to music—such as "Papo Tres," "Olga Pecho," "Juana Bochisme," "Tito Madera Smith" and other "Jewels" extracted from barrio sidewalks and tenement kitchens.

But we are in the "enclave," Latin New York 1981, and it's a wonder how deep those *plena* roots must run not simply to fade off into the cultural ferment of *salsa*, Nuyorican poetry and disco rap. An enclave is "n. a country [like Puerto Rico], or esp. an outlying portion of a country [like the Puerto Rican colony in New York], entirely or mostly surrounded by the territory of another country [the U.S.]." It means to be enclosed, locked in (originally "clave" referred to both lock and key). But when they threw away the key Tato picked up on it, striking up the "clave" within the enclave itself, sustaining its rhythmic and idiomatic heritages and tuning it in with whatever other snaps, beats and turns of phrase resound around it.

Out of the colonial enclave, then, there is arising this kind of new voice and vision, steadfast in its emphasis on cultural origins and historical perspective yet always springing confinement, breaking the past open to contemporary and emergent resources of expression. It is integrally bilingual, not just Spanish plus English but an entire fabric of meaning composed of the semantic, phonetic and musical suggestiveness of both. "Enclave" is also "en clave," "song" is also how to pronounce "son" in English, "cantos negros" is Tato's preferred phrase for what is usually called "poesía negroide," and indeed "cantos negros" is not only more mellifluous but makes it meaningful, again, to readers in the "other" language.

Tato's "songs and cantos" are patriotic, to be sure, proudly and unmistakably Puerto Rican in humor and claim. But as is clear from the sequence of "Oro in Gold," instead of "patria y amor" this time *amor* comes first, poems like "flutist" and especially "sand," subtle conjurings of love, passionate, personal and world-wide. It is what Tato calls "ay bendito humanity," the sympathy that all peoples feel as it beats in

6

the heart of the Puerto Rican. Listen to how Tato ends his little poem "puerto rican" and you'll know what we mean:

> how
> highly
> we
> claim
> our
> worth
> conceiving
> new
> society
> inside
> cemented
> hard
> core
> beauty
> chanting
> snapping
> beats

Keep snapping, Tato!

Juan Flores
Centro de Estudios Puertorriqueños
City University of New York

Feelings of One

jorge brandon

poetry is an outcry, love, affection,
a sentiment, a feeling, an attitude,
a song.

it is internal gut expressing intimate
thoughts upon a moment's experience.

poetry is the incessant beauty called
a person by an action that takes form.

the smell of sand in water digging moon
the loving smile.

poetry is the mountain, the recital,
the reaction, the desire, to feel
right in wrong, to taste bitter
memory, to praise death, to mourn,
to call.

poetry, oh, poetry:

beautiful novels in short lived prose.

long live your concise aristocracy!

long live your detailed concrete forms!

long live the people who espouse you!

long live sentiments of love!

long live unending desires, on and on
forever on:

poetry poetry

a poeta called

the soul!

jesús papote

It was untouched energy that reached
the shakings of his embryonic testicles
he moved eyes closed body crouched face
inside her body nobody knew his identity
not even his name he laid inside casket
corpse brethren woman strung out deep
cornered jungle streets eyes closed body
crouched face tucked pregnant belly sali-
vating umbilical cord peddling multi-
cut heroin sub-ghetto fortress chanting
early winter 25 degree cold-frío shivering
lacked attention lacked warmth born-to-be
embryo asphyxiated 25 dollars powers pene-
trating veins venas veins venas pouring
rivers pouring up mountain muscles brain's
tributaries.

She allowed herself to be touched old men
seeking last minute enjoyment thrills
social security military retirement pensions
on the woman about to give birth body running
down 13th street looking desperately for the
fix the fix hope-esperanza fix satisfaction
she tripped pained herself bleeding internally
the water bag had broken she did not care her
jugular veins were asking for attention to be
fed intravenously that was her priority to
satisfy her veins pinpointed needle metal rape
open pores scar-burnt hands.

She reached 1980 lower east side's 9th street going
up down empty cellars abandoned building
drug hideouts sad desperation christmas eve
thighs scratching up down abandoned lot she
met the fix la cura the fix la cura cura cura
she escaped stars relaxation she dreamt opium
drug re-leaving her into fantasy world beyond

universe still body mind ecstasy diluted chem-
icals soothing pain in brain she felt no body
no-motion-body knocked by powerful earthly drug
heroin she wanted heroin yes yes she wished
she loved heroin slow motion ejaculations
exploding nervous system open-preyed flesh human
body not feeling dry winter air christmas eve
noche buena 12 o'clock tranquility night of peace
no mangers night of hope heroin reaching embryo
about-to-be-born little child silent night feeding
tubes struggling to survive being born to die
pneumonia choking or overdosed body 12 o'clock
abandoned lot dying fire all by himself alone:

He was born star of peace church bells
he was born busting out loud cry church bells
he was born son grand son great grand son
he was born generations america puerto rico
he was born europe africa 7 generations before
he was born latest legacy family tree inheritor
he was born he was born 20th century
urban story greatest told abandonment
concrete land new york city story of stories
contemporary poets felt the spirit in the air
those who searched for lost souls new prophecies
celebrating jesus christ one thousand nine hun-
dred and eighty times seeking christ spirit
ritual midnight mass family dinners children
fast asleep santa claus is coming silent night
holy night he pushed an echo into death's eulogy
one speech one experience one smell one feeling
one moment one look one touch one breath one cry
one prayer "i am jesús i have no last name so call
me jesús papote" his first words unnoticed by bells
midnight bells christmas day alley cat licking
wombs she slept she never felt maternal instinct
ultimate pain released for only she could give birth
for only she could experience red faced explosions
elevated to that sacrificial offering called life

vida life vida life vida death life death new birth
abraham sacrificed consciously she sacrificed sub-
consciously invisible ancestor of soledad he spoke:

My name is jesús papote i am born in oppression
my death a deeper martyrdom unknown to pain to
solitude to soledad to soledad's seven skins to
darkness to darkness' mystery to mystery's spirits.

My name is jesús papote i live nine months gut soul
i was addicted i was beaten i was kicked i was punched
i slept in empty cellars broken stairways i was infect-
ed i was injected spermed with many relations
i ran from police jails i was high every day of life
stabbing murders 1980 20th-century moon rockets micro-
magnetic computer operations 120-story edifices united
states instant replay future 21st-century advanced
new york the world lives in 1970 new york underdevel-
oped world in 1960 new york i am in 1980 new york
born around 18-century abandoned structures
fighting to prevent broken scars from creating cancer
to my death.

My name is jesús papote born holy saturday easter
sunday march mother parading 3rd avenues' lower
streets car horns how much how long hotels
parking lots cellars men women elders new jersey
staten island connecticut long island all entered
my mother's secret veins 10 dollars 15 dollars i
was created ethnic sperm consortium's passionless
thrills social club more men entering more men en-
tering i was conceived easter sunday resurrection
pagan abuses 1980 modern times.

She awoke she felt strange she relaxed the fix
had been applied nodding dance completed she
visited grandmother daisy flowers she could be
normal for a while folkloric mountain music

i met grandmother on my first day what an omen
grandma abuelita can you see me grandmother i
was the answer to your prayers your many unan-
swered prayers grandma i am alive can you see me
abuelita insisted to stay easter sunday veins
were pumping they take no vacation she had to
make the streets she walked past gossip's stares
abuelita felt ashamed abuelita felt herself no-
body she had failed her daughter's baptism con-
firmation communion dignity pride virginity left
behind but she prayed even harder faith almighty
god not diminished candles the seven powers pro-
mises abuelita prayed her prayers made it easy
tonight . . . food rest spring walk she had to fight
the street she had refused the pimp's protection
she had to fight the corner she had no friends
she felt free tonight's crosscurrents open ethnic
music she felt something strange inside she walked
the glorious town central park rides broadway
nights bridges she looked across the waters ferry
evening lights statue of liberty's torch carrying
hand so strong wall street sunday silent newspaper
tonight tomorrow village open sexual society she
opinionated she knew new york's empty crevices
camera eyes recorded the instinct she felt strange
she felt something inside.

My name is jesús papote may month flowers she dis-
covered me making her green throwing up she wanted
abortion she took pill after pill she had to wait
syphilis infection i came between the habit she
needed more i was an obstruction constant pressure
wrinkled inside cars in out constant pounding those
men were paying they had a right to hurt the habit
stronger tricks longer she became oral more and more
the money was not there one night nobody wanted her
she decided to extricate me she pounded punch after
punch like those men punch after punch abortion at
all costs she tired herself i lost my voice i support-

ed her she was weak she could not move sitting
sidewalk cold cement she laid in bowery vagabonds
feeling her for nothing this was it she wanted no
more no more.

My name is jesús papote june cold turkey center cold
turkey her system must contain itself without chemi-
cals cold turkey naked unseasoned no taste unfeathered
cold turkey dry frozen human force battle begun fight
sweat shivers attacks in all directions cold turkey
intravenous coup d'etat demanding charging torturing
nuclear blasts invasions delirium opiate roots electric
shocks kidnapping she threw up the world she greened
she scratched-drew-blood nails on scars scabbing
pores blood vessels eruptions hands on blood she
painted open mental torture digging into wall's
electricity cabled concussion paralyzing currents
she wrote god let me die god let me die she fought
we fought i was not an added burden i kept quiet
i held if she survived detoxified normal life no
more deserted streets no more pains no more misery
she won grandma she won she smiled she ate she
beat the odds.

My name is jesús papote 4th of July celebration
plane ride across to puerto rico mountain house
utuado high up clear nights future dreams new
life breathings caribbean enchanted nation long
rides past guajataca splendored beaches arecibo's
indian caves dorado evenings she entered san juan
white cemetery patriots resting singing to la
perla pearled down old spanish architecture el
morro distanced open sea curving palm trees tick-
ling skies connecting sea-breezing moon san juan
song folklore painting after painting came alive
leo-mildness-august night tidal waves moving bells
quietly sunset lowering her thighs cooled refreshed
stimulated sauna touches moon-lit beauty mark smiled
sun met in ocean eclipse mistress round-up night

16

after night shimmering fresh air slow pace coastal
sand walk fresh fruit pineapple spicy fish coconut
nights kissing early morning mango blossoms new sun
octapusing rays orange rainbows the ox-cart was your
solution your final triumph how beautiful you look
inside the western sunset phosphorous bay shining
artesian ponce musically carved saints flamboyant
trees luquillo beach preparations into rain forest
deities once lived they greet us they talk loíza
carnaval blackness río grande julia de burgos phras-
ings oh mamita i was so afraid oh mamita stay in
taíno mountains caguana-shaped symbol of cemí oh
mamita don't go back give birth in island nativeness
tropical greetings nurturing don't go back don't
go back.

My name is jesús papote september pregnant body new
york spells trouble once-again-racing-fast struggles
rapid fire pellets struggles pouring anxieties 18th
century remnants immigrant struggles spanish second
third class citizens struggles education non-existent
struggles companion song of destiny struggles spell
troubles.

My name is jesús papote she october tried training
program cellar jobs she vowed not to use it again
columbus was discovered he discovered gold discov-
ered competition discovered defeat discovered lack
of opportunity halloween witch creeping in she said
no she said no strong they came back she said no
strong ugly cursed evil she said no strong she felt
pains i was restless i was acting up i had relapsed
i was choking i needed it she said no she said no
strong i was in pain she said no yes no yes no no
urgings yes yes achings no no yes no yes no yes
stubbornly she said no she said no she said no
strong.

My name is jesús papote november all souls day

grandma knocked on door oh no the prayers fell
defeated once again pain killers sleeping face
hallway scrambling avenues putrid dope stumbles
nightsticks digging digging deep spinal corded
night 300 dollars pure divinity bombarded atomic
explosions final war coma death radiation pellets
death la muerte sneaking in no breath feelings
death la muerte coming after us moving fast
death la muerte assured us she was winning
death la muerte doctors priests last testament
death la muerte trying to save me over my mother
death la muerte she refused her strength engulfed
death la muerte doorbell of fear
death la muerte abusing us unfairly
death la muerte nothing could be done
death la muerte divine hope of all living things
death was spitting its steel claws earthquake
we attacked her we fought her we prevented her
from penetrating our testicles we pulled her
intestines her naked slimy body we switch bladed
cuts across her face we rumbled into her adam's
apple biting into her senses we squeezed her
obnoxious overweight loose teeth cancer we cut her
breasts we raped her we mugged her we escaped her we
iced her thanksgiving fiesta carved with delight
we were eating seasoned turkey triumph champagne
toast to that ultimate desire to live live vivir.

My name is jesús papote december christmas new
york city my inner cycle 9 months completed what
a life what a life my mother's mouth once again
on elder's variety theatre 2 dollars 40 mouths
every day christmas eve day oh sweet sour destiny
ghetto sacrifice wounded limbs tears surfacing
loneliness soledad seven skins solitude underneath
sub-vulgate open concubines society condones it
society has not cured itself from it society cannot
outlaw such misery right there for future children
to see to watch to fear right there in front of

18

little angels in naked open spaces oh but sad lonely
night dear saviour's birth long lay the world in
sin 'til he appeared thrill of hope save him jesus
alleycats symphony save him jesus abandoned tenement
screaming save him jesus indians buried inside cement
chanting save him jesus she did not hear final cry:

Mami Mami push push i'm coming out celestial barkings
Mami Mami push i don't want to die she slept
Mami Mami push i want to live she slept cough
Mami Mami i have the ability to love cough cough
Mami Mami fight with me again she slept she slept
Mami Mami i'm coming out out out push push push push
Mami Mami can you feel me can you hear me push push
push push empuja empuja cough cough push push push
empuja empuja Mami cough cough push push i am fighting
i am fighting push push nature nature i have a will
to live to denounce you nature i am fighting by myself
your sweeping breasts your widowing backbone
yearnings your howling cemetery steps your
death-cold inhuman palms Mami Mami wake up
this is my birthday little mornings king
david sang cough cough cough push push
why do I have to eulogize myself
nobody is listening i am invisible
why tell me why do i have to be
the one the one to acclaim that:

    We, nosotros, compassionate caring people
    We, nosotros, respectful of spanish-english forms
    We, nosotros, peace in mind tranquility
    We, nosotros, inside triangle of contradictions
    We, nosotros, nation-feeling-total-pride
    We, nosotros, strong men powerful women loving children
    We, nosotros, hispanic hemispheric majority
    We, nosotros, latinos million bicultural humanists
    We, nosotros, folkloric mountain traditionalists
    We, nosotros, spanish tongue culture older than english
    We, nosotros, conceiving english newer visions

We, nosotros, multi-ethnic black-brown-red in affirmations
We, nosotros, ghetto brothers black americans indians
           italians irish jewish polish ukrainians
           russian german food and music lovers
We, nosotros, mathematicians of the magical undocumented
           dollar architects of close-knit spaces
We, nosotros, 5th largest foreign market we consumed
           all the goods 83 years association of
           goods we fought world wars decorated up
           front to meet the fresh-troop enemy
We, nosotros, oral poets transcending 2 european forms
           spanish dominance when spanish was strong
           english dominance when english was strong
           we digested both we absorbed the pregnancies
           we stand at crossroads 21st-century new man
           great grandfathers chornos-spirits sing
           with me allow me this one last wish limbo
           baptism of faith this one last christmas
           moment to my mother who doesn't answer

with the permission of all the faiths of all beliefs
with the permission of this land
with the permission of the elders
with the permission of english
with the permission of my community
with the permission of god:

   allow this spanish word to be understood
   i ask for your silence for language is
   always understood in any sentiment
   with your permission Mami
   i ask for one gift one magi gift
   inside these heavy odds
   there is a spanish word
   spanish ultimate of words
   that will survive
   there is a puerto rican
   blessing universal to the world
   hear it it is only for you

for i love you i don't blame you
i am also responsible for state
of being, so with this, my only
breath, my last wind, my last
supper sentiment, i tell you
with pride that i am proud to
have been your son, to have come
from you, with the tenderness
of my grandmother's prayers,
with the silent love of all my
people, with the final resolution
of our nationhood, i am asking
for my blessings BENDICION
BEN . . . DI . . . CI . . . ON

she woke up she saw she startled she warmed she
protected she cried she broke the umbilical cord
she got up to follow the bells the bells the bells
cats dogs vagabonds all followed the tinkle tinkle
of the bells christmas bells nativity flowing bells
faith hope and charity bells 1980 jesus christ and
jesús papote midnight ecstacy of bells church steps
door opens organ stops up the aisle she exclaimed
jesús papote human legacy god the son at the right
hand holy spirit candles flowers incense wine water
and finally the people grandmother she offered jesús
papote to the people miracle cherubims flautists
dancing and singing rejoice rejoice eternity smiles
oh night divine oh night divine she knelt she smiled
jesús papote's presence in the dignity of our lives.

little man

awfully quiet this saturday morning
americanita placing book on shelves
she observed up-tight librarian
divinity-walking air sternly
out the central door.

awfully quiet this saturday morning
americanita alone except for little man
it was so secretive so quiet
so out of touch with neighborhood
so old so pretty so well preserved
so mysterious so beautifully lonely
so silent that . . .
they kissed
and tongue kissed
and played with fingers
so quietly romantic
underneath the literature section
carrying-on worthy of
instant chapters
library tabernacles
pleasing with delight . . .

serious dude

Yes, sí, i like her, y qué,
what's wrong with that?
I don't care who she's in love with,
i'm in love with her,
i'm not going to deny it, bro,
yo no lo voy a negar, so what, so,
i'll never kiss her, that's okay too,
but i dig the way she walks,
i mean she walks like finger-snapping
church bells on summer conga drums
playing clave on time, yes, sí
i want her, y qué, it's not her,
it's me, it's my fantasies, bro,
it's what turns me on, it's about
my dreams, and so what if she never
kisses me, hey, you can't have every-
thing, but i know one thing, she'll
live with my memory, i'm not afraid
to tell her that i love her, i want
her to feel strong and secure, i
want her to feel strong and secure,
that somebody likes her, you dig,
whoever likes her will know that
i like her too, and when she looks
at herself, she'll know i'm there,
bro, and, in her private moments,
i know i make her happy, you dig,
i know because i'm bad, that's why,
because i treat her with respect,
that's why, and i live with la
esperanza, hey, that one day, un día,
she will walk my proud jitterbug
down this vecindario, brother-man,
i'm waiting, bro, i'm waiting, bro,
this is soul gut, my man, so
remember, if she wants me, i expect
you to step aside, bro, i mean that,
serious.

tito madera smith
(for Dr. Juan Flores)

he claims he can translate palés matos'
black poetry faster than i can talk,
and that if i get too smart,
he will double translate pig latin
english right out of webster's
dictionary, do you know him?

he claims he can walk into east harlem
apartment where langston hughes gives
spanglish classes for newly-arrived
immigrants seeking a bolitero-numbers
career and part-time vendors of cuchi-
fritters sunday afternoon in central
park, do you know him?

he claims to have a stronghold of the
only santería secret baptist sect in
west harlem, do you know him?

he claims he can talk spanish styled in
sunday dress eating crabmeat-jueyes
brought over on the morning eastern
plane deep fried by la negra costoso
joyfully singing puerto rican folklore:
"maría luisa no seas brava,
llévame contigo pa la cama," or
"oiga capitán delgado, hey captain delgaro,
mande a revisar la grama, please inspect
the grass, que dicen que un aeroplano,
they say that an airplane throws marijuana
seeds."

do you know him? yes you do,
i know you know him, that's right,
madera smith, tito madera smith:

he blacks and prieto talks at the same time,
splitting his mother's santurce talk,
twisting his father's south carolina soul,
adding new york scented blackest harlem
brown-eyes diddy bops, tú sabes mami,
that i can ski like a bomba soul salsa
mambo turns to aretha franklin stevie
wonder nicknamed patato guaguancó steps,
do you know him?

he puerto rican talks to las mamitas
outside the pentecostal church, and
he gets away with it, fast-paced i
understand-you-my-man, with clave
sticks coming out of his pockets hooked
to his stereophonic 15-speaker indispensable
disco sounds blasting away at cold reality
struggling to say estás buena baby
as he walks out of tune and out of
step with alleluia cascabells,
puma sneakers,
pants rolled up,
shirt cut in middle chest,
santería chains,
madamo pantallas,
into the spanish social club,
to challenge elders in dominoes,
like the king of el diario's
budweiser tournament
drinking cerveza-beer
like a champ,
do you know him?
well, i sure don't,
and if i did, i'd
refer him to 1960
social scientists
for assimilation
acculturation
digging
autopsy

into
their
heart
attacks,
oh,
oh,
there
he
comes,
you can call him tito,
or you can call him madera,
or you can call him smitty,
or you can call him mr. t.,
or you can call him nuyorican,
or you can call him black,
or you can call him latino,
or you can call him mr. smith,
his sharp eyes of awareness,
greeting us in aristocratic harmony:
"you can call me many things, but
you gotta call me something."

juana bochisme

ay virgen, mira que si fulana de tal estaba anoche
con juan de los parlotes, metida en un carro y,
tú sabes, la dejaron a tres cuadras de la esquina,
dicen que era el boss de la factoría,
y lo más peor, salió con las, tú sabes, toda estrujá. . . .
santa maría purísima, y que pegándole cuernos al pobre juan pueblo
simplemente porque lo vio salir de una barra a las tres de la mañana,
esa escusa como que no suena bien ¿verdad?
en serio, no te miento, carlos cocina le metió tremenda pescosá
en pleno baile porque bailó merengue con un dominicano,
eso le pasa por ser presentá. . . .
y la victoria ascensor, me dijo manny parque
que lo oyó de tito esquina que lo habían llamado de puerto rico,
te lo juro, lo que pasa en nueva york inmediatamente lo saben en manatí,
se me perdió el hilo . . . sí, ajá, es así,
¿te das cuenta del revolú con pedro edificio?
la rosa cuarto sin vergüenza lo choteó con el housing
de su jugada de gallo en el quinto piso de los proyectos,
pero existe un detalle que no está claro,
según las lenguas por ahí,
me dijeron del bochinche con estrella avenida,
esa mujer rompecasa fuerza de cara corteja de pablo escalera,
¿puedes tú creer semejante cosa?
ella le quita los cheques del social security
mientras vive con pedro rufo en un hotel de brooklyn,
y le saca otro cheque a la welfare con una dirección de staten island . . .
y ¿qué me dices de la petra sala?, tiene una tienda de food stamps,
se ha hecho millonaria vendiendo bolita en tres condados,
guiada de viuda, soltera y divorciá,
comprando casa en puerto rico sin pagar presupuestos,
y si tú la vieras, la llorona teresa azotea,
pues, ahora te cuento, fíjate,
le quitó los chavos al enclenco flaco aquel que estaba en la fiesta,
¿te recuerdas?, sí, ése mismo, óyeme,
y después lo amenazó con el bartender mafioso del social club,
hijo de uno de sus queridos, amigo de su ex-amante,
con tanto revolú y traqueteo, no sabes tú el dolor de cabeza

que a mí me da para memorizarme el garabato pan de gato
que existe en el tercer piso de mi edificio,
te digo que el welfare me debe pagar overtime. . . .
pero no te he contado el último descaro,
mario se viste de maría cuando viene el social worker,
y jesús acera me dijo que la pepa bolita
hizo un brujo con una haitiana,
¿sabes para quién?, imagínate tú, pues, para mí,
ella dijo que yo era una lengüilarga, si yo fuera lengüilarga
te diría que ella es una marimacha apestosa, pero yo,
inmediatamente me fui a la espiritista y me limpié,
por eso vine aquí primero a contarte todo esto,
ya que no te gusta hablar pero que te encanta oír,
bueno, me voy, ay virgen, si ya es tiempo de cocinar,
tengo que avanzar, me esperan en el 360, el 430 y pico,
la bodega, la lavandería, tendré que hablar entre novelas,
cómo se va el tiempo, dios santo.

unemployment line

pablo pueblo city man, unemployed man, stands 20th in line,
pablo pueblo city man, unemployed man, stands 15th in line,
pablo pueblo city man, unemployed man, stands 5th in line,
pablo pueblo city man, unemployed man, stands first in line,
on the unemployment circle:

    ¿usted me puede atender?
    ¿usted me puede atender?
    he esperado en esta línea,
    y aunque yo no sepa inglés,
    deme deme el privilegio,
    de acercarme hacia usted,
    oiga usted, me puede atender,
    un trabajo yo quiero obtener,

    yo vengo de la cantera,
    por el paso de un avión,
    aquí en el sur bronx llegué,
    a buscar una fortuna,
    y aprender un poco inglés,
    oiga usted, ¿me puede atender?

    me mandaron aquí ayer,
    me mandaron allá antier,
    y antes de ayer, el mes se fue,
    pasaron tres, ya tengo diez,
    me encuentro abajo y deprimido,
    oiga usted, ¿me puede atender?

    ¿usted me puede atender?
    ¿usted me puede atender?
    ¿usted me puede atender?

    después de esta letanía,
    hablé con la señorita de este bembé,
    y ella con una risa que no era linda,
    con una gracia que era maldita,

me dijo así, así, así:
"please speak in english
speak english sir,
don't understand a word you say,
speak english sir,
don't understand a word you say."

¿usted me puede atender?, me caso en diez,
¿usted me puede atender?, me caso en diez,
basta ya, atiéndame,
basta ya, atiéndame,
atiéndame, atiéndame,
basta ya.

pablo pueblo city man, unemployed man, stands outside
the unemployment circle, they made a check for him
on the spot.

bolita folktale

one-thirty south bronx tale took form,
don julio silently dreamed, "pegarse"
feelings digested in "pensamientos,"
paradise bar otb/numbers don q conversations,
pedro jukebox navaja blading latino tragedy.

two-thirty el barrio tale took form,
el mudo rushed into paradise bar,
nine fingers in the air, "el nueve,"
don julio's good luck dream,
927 san juan street,
don julio woke to play 927 today.

three-thirty brooklyn tale took form,
el mudo rushed into paradise bar,
two fingers in the air, "el dos,"
tension in don julio's smile,
bolita payoffs on number 2 at 8 to 1,
brooklyn, manhattan, múcura at night,
don julio had the 927 going,
bruni the barmaid excited,
the smell of 1000 "pescados" at stake,
rounds of "salud, buena suerte, agua
florida, santa bárbara" crossing
fingers for number 7 to come out.

four-thirty loisaida tale took form,
el mudo rushed into paradise bar,
seven fingers in the air, "el siete,"
don julio's back gleefully showered
with "aprietos" peeling open bar,
free drinks, kissing cheeks, many
payoffs on lucky 7 at 8 to 1,
el mudo jumping and dancing,
he took the number, hotel will be paid.

five-thirty new york spinal corded,
celebration turned sour, Pedro el
Bolitero came in, not feeling ecstatic,
quickly reminding don julio, the 927
was for manhattan, he played brooklyn,
drowning jubilation turned apologetic
broken pockets lifetiming "ava maría,
qué mala suerte, por poco, por un hilo,
no te apures, juega
combinao la próxima vez, la suerte te
vendrá, ten fe, ya tú verás."

six o'clock south bronx tale took form,
don julio playing 927 for manhattan múcura,
thinking of a smarter bet, another dream,
the better odds, inside the sunset of a
new york city night.

abandoned building

LA VIDA es un español derretido
        un frío escalofrío
        donde el sol solamente
        acaricia mi rota realidad
        reñida entre la
        urbe americana y
        un barrio corazón
        latino.

LA VIDA es un folklore de pueblo
        jíbaro encarretado en
        televisiones dominadas
        del sabor ron coca-cola
        bolita bachata juego y
        sudor.

LA VIDA es una derrota en la escuela
        un sobretrabajo mal pagado
        un amor tierno y fuerte
        donde las necesidades se
        vacían en el cuerpo de
        la esperanza.

LA VIDA es un inglés frío
        un español no preciso
        un spanglish disparatero
        una insegurida de
        incendios automáticos.

LA VIDA es pues, mi pana, LA VIDA es
        un dolor de muela
        mellada en el hueco
        seno cáncer, sin remedio,
        parada en el cemento,
        de esta triste,
        mi desnuda realidad.

olga pecho

yo me batallo
con la vida
apuesto 200 pesos
cuando viene el cheque
yo me vuelvo loca
jugando barajas
hasta que me esnúen
black jack por chupones
si sale 21 a mano negra
tengo que meterle mano
a la jodedera en las
azoteas del basement
con el corazón empinao
a lo cool-cool marimacha
del destino.
si gano gano si pierdo
pues pierdo pero hay
que tirarse a pecho hay
que jugarse la vida el
primero del mes de todos
los días yo me las juego
con cualquiera.
ya la gente me respeta
saben que no hay más na.

maría ciudad

era la luz de la mañana,
triste y sola se encontraba,
otro día, mil apuros,
otro día, sin descanso.

en su reflección ella buscaba,
fuerza, aliento, en su espada,
para batallar la vida entera
hasta papel de hombre ella jugaba.

a las potencias les rogó,
se llenó de inspiración,
a sus hijos levantó,
a la escuela, a su futuro.

maquinillando se encontró,
trabajó con mucho orgullo,
era la fuente de energía,
y sus compañeros, así se lo decían:

maría en las ciudades, fuerte se veía
confrontaba las situaciones,
llena en progreso, llena de vida.

almorzaba en el teléfono,
cuentas a plazo, cuido en niños,
a las cinco ella corría
a preparar la cena,
y adorar a sus hijos,
y el sol, el sol, el sol medio dormido,
maría ciudad, a ella admiró,
con su rojo colorido,
por las calles le cantó:

maría en las ciudades, fuerte se veía,
confrontaba las situaciones,
llena en progreso, llena de vida.

era dura, era fuerte,
era brava y protectiva,
el amor si viene viene,
después que mis deberes
estén cumplidos,
en la noche descanso,
se miró en su reflección,
y aquí lo íntimo llegó,
y a su amante ella llamó.

maría en las ciudades, fuerte se veía,
confrontaba las situaciones,
llena en progreso, llena de vida:

¡maría ciudad!
¡maría ciudad!
¡maría ciudad!

puerto rican

silk
smooth
ivory
polished
into
brown
tan
black
soul
leaning
back
looking
proud
sharp
answers
casual
community
conversations
based
in
mental
admiration
how
highly
we
claim
our
worth
conceiving
new
society
inside
cemented
hard
core
beauty
chanting
snapping
beats

familia

moment's personal worth,
life ceases for a minute,
pays attention to a milestone.

moments when choke of tear,
adams apple above the eye.

moments when sacrifices find glory.

moments when we come together,
everlasting kinship strength.

moments when ay bendito humanity
flourishes and expands.

and of course,

moments when family tree
sees nuclear-expanded
attention moving upward,
abuelita at the center
of the trust.

sky people
(la gente del cielo)

Eye-scratching mountain view
Puerto Rico counting houses
upon houses, hill after hill,
in valleys and in peaks,
to observe: la gente del cielo,
fingering on clouds,
climbing further and further,
to preserve taíno folklore,
gente del cielo,
toiling the land,
artcrafting musical symbols,
giving birth to more angelitos del cielo,
whose open-spaced hands captured moon waltz:
solemn serenity serenading life,
la gente del cielo,
who prayed in nature's candlelight,
galaxies responding with milky way guiñaítas
winked in tropical earth smile,
as God gleefully conceded,
what we had perceived all along,
that Puerto Rico is 100 by 35 by 1000
mountains multiplied by the square root
of many cultures breathing: ONE.

diega

diega llega, diega arrives, diega legacies,

diega llega, diega portrays, diega street-smarts,

diega llega, diega understands, diega loves. . . .

what more can i say about your soft strokes
caricias screaming gently on a smile.

what more can i say about your gracious
saludos hometown sentimientos mountain
jibarita romantic melody of songs streaming
from your lips memories yearning from your
soul.

what more can i say, diega, how easy to say
your name, tu nombre, no pretensions, no
ornaments, saying simply diega, easy to
reach, easy to touch, dulce-soft silk
embroidered symphony your voice chanting
dancing living a call, your call, diega.

diega, you have arrived a otra etapa,
another time, but need not worry mamita,
you can sing to us the winds at night
are waiting, and we will speak your
caring phrases protecting our hands,
inspiring our eyes, stimulating our
senses.

diega, woman, mother, simplicity in
every sound you syllabled to us,
what more, diega, what more than
essence kissing petals on our
foreheads, never to be forgotten
affection, the rivers, the mountains,

the heavens, you touched us, you hugged
us, deeply, freely, diega, diega,
we respect your presence,
your children grandchildren
tátaranietos and chornos of the future........

te recordamos en el presente, bendición,
vieja, you diega, opening the door of
st. peter, festive celebration in the
gates of your eternity and this Barrio
that you touched.

Oro in Gold

flutist

she
sprayed
golden
syllables
angelic
whistle
calls
gently
phrasing
musical
notes
fingering
celestial
innocence
inside
warm
lonely
nights
waiting
for
the
serenade

sand

finely grained
crystals sea-polished
weightless granules
salt water aging rocks
planted smoothly
naked grounds
inviting evening's
open bosoms
flawless winds
riding breezes
tidal waves
mistress
lover-nights
shaped mountain
craters moon-love
yearnings
pregnant
nature's
many periods
virgin fragility
as in french
talk making
love.

just before the kiss

canela brown sugar coated bomboncitos
melting deliciously upon a sweet tooth tongue;
canela brown gold dust on top of tembleque;
canela brown fine sticks to flavored cocoa;
canela grounded into arroz con dulce;
canela melao
canela dulce.

canela browned in deep tan caribbean
sweet lips almost sabroso tasted by
a cariñoso sentiment, y buena que estás,
en gusto affection that cries
out loud: qué chévere tú eres,
como canela brown warrior woman diplomática
with her terms.

all of this canela,
inside your luscious lips,
smooth phrasing me deeeeply,
waking me up on the middle-night,
to change from exclamation mark
into an accent accenting:
canela, mi negra,
canela, trigueña,
canela, mulata,
canela, mi prieta,
bésame,
to taste your
cinnamon
powdered
tongue.

standards

in order for you to touch me,
you would have to convince me,
you respect my all, my ambitions,
my beliefs, for you to touch me,
you must allow freedom to my space,
you must express human sincerity,
detest gluttony and greed,
but if i say touch me,
you have won my heart,
i will take your universe beyond,
i will talk incessantly into your ears,
i will caress your limb's existence,
so suave, touch,
so smooth, touch, touch,
sweet
smells
sensored
sensual
sensations
saturated
softly
smoothly
seducing
sensitive
stems
slowly

scenting
sensuous
touch, oh, touch, deep in
            divino, divina,
            qué bueno

libertad

velluda: alliterated y eslembao

it was all about my fingers, each one of them:
    el meñique se figuraba fuerte
    fabulosamente fermentando figuras
    fraternales en el rocío de tu boca.
it was all about my fingers, each one of them:
    el anular circulando cuadros
    concéntricos cariñosamente
    caminando por el pecho en tus
    montañas.
it was all about my fingers, each one of them:
    el del corazón suavizando sen-
    sualmente sobos sexuales suspirando
    en las venas de tu vientre.
it was all about my fingers, each one of them:
    el índice lubricando lazos lucientes
    en las ramas de tus piernas.
and finally, mi negra,
it was all about my fingers, each one of them:
    el pulgar hincándose íntimamente
    ilustrándose en las bases de
    tus raíces.
i came down, all the way down,
completing nurture
then you, mulata, you gave
birth to my hands, which
you caressed until the
touches tinkled stars of
delight as you introduced
me to your universe:
    velluda: alliterated y eslembao,
    i got lost inside your rain forest.

the patria in my borinquen

that i stumbled into my spring walk
wrinkled seven years many night brawls
marijuanated lover calls forcing you
to give it up give it all up your
poetry drowsing passionless pleasures
scar-faced avenue walk.

all of a sudden i met my puppy love
across the street washed up skinny
body i searched searched transformed:

> teenage summer central park
> in my eyes you aristocratic virgin
> in your eyes me creative wind
> we exchange love poems
> i gave in you gave in you
> undid me i trembled the numbered
> poems delicate poetic spanglish
> grammatically sensing me
> you bit i bit we bit the grass
> your lips gave me puertoricanness
> intimately transformed transformed:

i face your loisaida air struggling to move
bones crushing facing adversity hard times
suffering times, and for a macho moment i
thought i was your beauty your positive
strength i went after you running screaming
liberating your chains, "patria, you are my
borinquen; patria, your are my borinquen,"
you turned around, my spirit felt relaxed,
you were strong enough to overcome all
obstacles, mi patria, and still leave
borinquen taína poetry to
caress heart world

penetration
(to sandra esteves/julia de burgos)

the day julia de burgos came back
to project herself into modern existence
to announce sister-love for poet-woman
whose tranquility was amputated by a
riocheted bullet infiltrating spiritual
vibration bullet exploding in direction
of taína woman two children abreast
inside sad desperation abandoned building
caves only to miss the bus only to feel
mother-father struggles street-walking
alone.

> the day julia de burgos came back out
> of alcoholic liver busting along street
> corner resurrection was to intersect
> interject face hand heart rejecting
> pellets penetrating sandra's children
> skulls.

but sandra felt cone-shaped steel
penetrating soft-shelled skin
preventing her from carrying
children now astounded grimacing
pain mami's llantos lowering
face hand heart neck knees
surrendering petals demon's bite
blessing cold-deep sidewalk's
sorrowful turmoil.

> julia de burgos watched in pain
> remembering her day she inspired
> sandra to combat to denounce to
> demand thorough examination, no
> more wasteful deaths, no more
> bullets from destitute society,
> deaths will be natural, deaths
> will be patriotic confrontation.

then, julia de burgos went to
puerto rico, to lolita lebrón
novena-praying for many sandra
marías avenging in every medi-
tation in every act of life
the grips of those whose pellets
wanted to control puerto rican
women's self-destiny.

compañera
(for susana)

entre el conjunto, compañera,
el patriotismo-siempre-vive
en la historia puertorriqueña.

entre el sonido, compañera,
noches largas después del
trabajo atravezando barrios
llevando claridades puertorriqueñas.

entre comillas, compañera,
hablar claro poderoso
respeto de razas y cultura
nueva realidad puertorrinqueña.

entre mis frases, compañera,
sociedades libres de dueños
envidiosos.

entre la verda, sí, más que sí, compañera,
adentro de un festejo, dos vasos de vino,
dos fuertes abrazos, una comunidad
puertorriqueña.

y al fin,

        entre las gotas de sudor,
        entre el don de un amor fiel,
        entre el cariño libre de mentiras,
        entre el beso firme y sensual
        entre nuestros hermanos, compañera.

Prendas

alicia alonso

absolutamente
ascendiendo
acrobáticamente
al
aire
acariciando
abiertamente
al
amor
al
ayer
al
angel
arropado
antes
al
andar
habanero
amaneciendo
abajo
atendiéndo
al
amor

suni paz

el son y la paz
debajo se ven un
cello celando el
le lo lai como
si picasso hubiera
nacido en borinquen
tierra un cello cielo
jibarito llamando la
flauta que toque cayey
cibao andes panamá
venezuela méjico en
una sola nota de son
y paz debajo se ve un
cello cielo celando
como que el otoño no
existe porque suni
canta argentina por
los barrios de esperanza
que hasta la conga se
desviste desde el cielo
y descansa su dolor

vaya carnal

sabes, pinche, que me visto
estilo zoot suit marca de
pachuco royal chicano air
force montoyado en rojo
azul verde marrón nuevo
callejero chicano carnales
eseándome como si el ése ése
echón que se lanza en las
avenidas del inglés con
treinta millones de batos
locos hablando en secreto
con el chale-ése-no-la-chingues
vacilón a los gringos americanos,
¿sabes?, simón, el sonido del este,
el vaya, clave, por la maceta,
que forma parte de un fuerte
lingüismo, raza, pana, borinquen,
azteca, macho, hombre, pulmones
de taíno, de indios, somos
chicano-riqueños, qué curada,
simón, que quemada mi pana,
la esperanza de un futuro
totalmente nuestro,
tú sabes, tú hueles,
el sabor, el fervor del
vaya, carnal.

john forever
"ten minutes of silence." . . . yoko

poetry haiku lyrics

filled with universal stanzas

music mirrors depth in visions

bonded chains harmony;

morning lines rhythmic phrases

singing night stars beads of sorrows

sensing smiling spirit feelings

loving songs hearts at ease:

> john of peace, john of peace
> john of peace, john of peace
> john of peace, john of peace
> sing, sing, sing
> john of peace, john of peace
> john of peace, john of peace
> john of peace, john of peace
> john of peace, john of peace
> john of peace:
>
> john forever, we espouse you
> john forever, we espouse you
> john forever, we espouse you
> sing your songs
> deep john sing:

sunday vigil not to worship

but to light a burning candle

tender loving skies of people

praying peace world at ease

closing eyes in meditation

yearning love winds deep sensations

chanting, humming, singing, whispering,
many tongues in one breeze:

> john of peace, john of peace . . .
> john forever, we espouse you
> john forever, we espouse you
> john forever, we espouse you
> sing your songs
> deep john sing. . . .

miriam makeba

place choice seat struggle sings africa:
celestial adjectives trumpets announce her entrance
verbs god's actions conjunction mountains
nouns rained phrases people's interjections
unified inside adverbs her tongue.

prepositions souled third world exclamation
applauses pronouns inside voice vernacular
ten languages one tone nativeness royal
presence odaro-greetings first born oral
expressions genuflecting richness.

she soul flows way back beginning of color
blackness veined seven continents every-
thing complacent they brought original back
new faces disturbing devils prostitution
presenting different version original life
civilization beginning-noise alphabets were
noises before adam's apple colonizers
sacrificed seven natural elements water sun
fire storm day night moon death praised oya
ogoun ochoun obatalá elleggua changó yemayá
reactions closest to god nature cannot be
controlled she shakes foundations tears
underneath drums constantly beating sending
messages whooping voice angers soothes
satisfies voice wastes no words meaningless-
ness cleansed tones eyes hearts tongues
fingers emotions breathtaking swelling veins.

her mood softens transforms mountain scene
africa seething beauty shadows earth skies
sun arrive heaven grounds queen soul queen
gentleness queen freedom festac universal
nigeria looking soul people dreaming stars
god's warriors liberating black lands
transformation taking place majority rule

home rule africa of age spirits speak strong
leaders seven powers raging black red cannot
stumble nigeria proud concert singer roots
in ritual universally understood culture.

her ultimate song release promise movements
promise rootness promise physical sacrifice
death for love promise looking each other
profound togetherness making it in all ways
of love in all ways of love in all ways and
manners of capable love in all ways and
expressions physical to love in all physical
spiritual mannerisms describing love alone
under sole star africa.

rafa

as triangular ship deposited blacks
caribbean molasses deposited blacks
for slavery and cotton;

as black african preserved original
culture inside christianity he was
forced to swallow;

as the puerto rican challenged
drums to bomba step's endurance
strength drummers against dancers;

as they created plena rhythms
to news events on southern ponce
streets;

as they searched for recognition
since 1500 finally melting into
puerto rican folklore;

as it all came down to rafael
cortijo playing bomba and plena
many piñones of my childhood;

as he finally exploded 1960
ismael rivera sounds puerto
rican charts creating music
the world over;

as we search through plena history
there's a godfather-padrino-figure
humble but stubborn to his traditions;

as we detail contributions
so must we all stand
gracious ovation
rafael cortijo
unanimous consensus
puerto rican people.

juan boria

hay que comenzar, de negro prieto mulato,
caciques que se derriten bomba-plena tumbando;
sí, hay que comenzar, en voz celeste africana,
sol negrura borinqueña, compás de pueblo cantando;
sí, hay que comenzar, en noche misterio maraña,
cocolos tambores rezando, ritos trigueños asaltando;
sí, hay que comenzar, a piel de esquinillero,
al vaya folklore hermano, miren lo que trajo el barco,
un puertorro declamando, nació un negro, nació un negro,
nació estirao, vestido de blanco, sabe usted,
nació y que pitando él alabado del nalgueo,
la comadrona grita, "un milagro,"
señores nació recitando rumbeando,
miren se paró de paso a paso,
pique en punta, bailando mambo,
oigan, señores, la virgen bendice, "un milagro,"
el barrio entero gritando, santurce, ponce,
hasta el gallo cucuruqueando, vengan, está aquí,
el director ejecutivo de la bemba burocracia,
huracán en remolino, un nuevo diccionario,
casabes, jueyes, cerezas, cogen panderetas en manos,
al on de la o, en la e de la i, la u son-pulso del compás
a empezar, a terminar   juan juan
palesmatear y guillenear   juan juan
con su gracia, su sonrisa   juan juan
su alta voz de melodía   juan juan
que comience el festejo,
lechón, morcilla, alcapurrias,
guineítos, salmorejo, ron llave,
coquito, lechoza, pasteles,
bacalaítos, la yuca y el ñame,
que venga la serenata, noche santa,
el presidente-comandante-caballero,
recitando al todo negro,
de la cuna con sus versos.

homenaje a don luis palés matos

retumba el pasado presente prosa poesía
retumba el calor sudor vaivenes de cuero
salpicando mares olor tambor prieto quemao
orgullos cadereando acentos al español
conspiración engrasando ritmos pleneros
a la lengua española pa ponerle sabor.

pero que retumba en la tumba resbalando
pico pico tun tun de pasa áfrica se pierde
en puerto rico tirando pasos nichos a los santos
marcando al uno dos en tres por cuatro
que alientan los versos exaltan los salmos
despierta la clave chupando las cañas
pracutú-piriquín-prucú-tembandeando
el secreto máximo: que luis palés matos
tombien era grifo africano guillao de castellano.

   qué de blanco:

                    era un grifo babalao oba-rey guayamesano,
                    salió de *sspirita* mulata liberada,
                    fue un trabajo de pueblo una noche secreta,
                    cogieron un ñáñigo *sspiritu* lui,
                    que espiraba a ser blanco,
                    con un tumbao celestial lenguas doz razas,
                    lo bautizaron palés añadieron el matos,
                    dios la pava omnipresente sacude exprime:
                    el trabajo, antillano, carifricano,
                    afro-españolisao, manteca sal y vinagre, y
                    de pronto se despierta un alma, un alma,
                    que alientan los cuerpos, maniobrando,
                    cabecita pa arriba, manitas pa' lado,
                    deditos en clave, pechito pa fuera, y salió:

                    un negrindio sureño, rascacielo de mulato,
                    patología criolla, ogoun-ochoun de barrio,

otun-derecha de la danza,
caracol cangrejo yemayado,
conocedor imprudente africano,
usted y tenga poeta antillano,
betún del brillo borincano,
pracutú-priniquín-prucú-tembandeando
el secreto máximo: que luis palés matos
también era grifo africano guillao de castellano.

bomba, para siempre

bomba: we know we are electricity, we know we are a sun:
bomba: bring in the jazz, and merengue, blend africa:
bomba: puerto rican history for always, national pride:
bomba: cadera beats, afternoon heat, sunday beach:
bomba: we all came in, negritos bien lindos:
bomba: center space, intact beauty, rhythmic pride:
bomba: compose the cheo song lucecita sings curet smiles:
bomba: and once again bomba: se queda allí bomba:

un negrito melodía he came along,
improvising bomba drums on dancer's feet,
choral songs, sonero heat, snapping hands,
sweat at ease, melodía sang,
he sang like this:

se queda allí, se queda allí, se queda allí, es mi raíz.

los carimbos en sus fiestas, español era su lengua,
le ponían ritmo en bomba, a castañuelas de españa vieja.

se queda allí, se queda allí, se queda allí, es mi raíz.

betances abrió los pasos, los negros son ciudadanos,
esa noche tocaron bomba, para la danza puertorriqueña.

se queda allí, se queda allí, se queda allí, es mi raíz.

la bomba ya está mezclada con las rimas jibareñas,
hundida ella se encontraba, bailando plena borinquen tierra.

se queda allí, se queda allí, se queda allí, es mi raíz.

me hace cantar, me hace reír,
me pone contento, me siento feliz.

se queda allí, se queda allí, se queda allí, es mi raíz.

por el frío yo la canto, por los parques caminando,
siento el calor en mi cuerpo, mis huesos en clave,
me dan aliento.

se queda allí, se queda allí, se queda allí, es mi raíz.

roberto lleva sus chornos, a la luna de roena,
el futuro está bien claro, la bomba es base,
no hay quien la mueva.

métele encima el jazz, el rock o fox trot inglesa,
la bomba se va debajo, ay virgen no hay quien la mueva,
piñones baila de ponce, mayagüez con su lero,
cortijo es el padre, curet es el cura, maelo la canta,
roberto lo jura, se queda allí, la bomba vive en mí,
se queda allí, yo soy feliz, se queda allí, allí, allí

      and at the end of these songs,
      in praise of many beats,
      my heart can only say:
      se queda allí.

ARTE PUBLICO PRESS BOOKS

La Carreta Made a U-turn, by Tato Laviera.	ISBN 0-934770-01-8	$5
EnClave, by Tato Laviera.	ISBN 0-934770-11-5	$5
La Bodega Sold Dreams, by Miguel Piñero.	ISBN 0-934770-02-6	$5
On Call, by Miguel Algarín.	ISBN 0-934770-03-4	$5
Mongo Affair, by Miguel Algarín.	ISBN 0-934770-04-2	$5
Nosotros Anthology (Latino Literature from Chicago).	ISBN 0-934770-06-9	$7.50
Latino Short Fiction, eds. Dávila & Kanellos	ISBN 0-934770-07-7	$7.50
The Adventures of the Chicano Kid *and Other Stories,* by Max Martínez	ISBN 0-934770-08-5	$7.50
Spik in Glyph?, by Alurista.	ISBN 0-934770-09-3	$5
Mi querido Rafa, by Rolando Hinojosa.	ISBN 0-934770-10-7	$7.50
Mujeres y agonías, by Rima Vallbona.	ISBN 0-934770-12-3	$5
Thirty 'n Seen a Lot, by Evangelina Vigil.	ISBN 0-934770-13-1	$5
El hombre que no sudaba, by Jaime Carrero.	ISBN 0-934770-14-x	$7.50
Kikirikí: Stories and Poems in *English and Spanish for Children,* edited by Sylvia Peña.	ISBN 0-934770-15-8	$7.50

Send Orders To
Arte Publico Press
Revista Chicano-Riqueña
University of Houston
Central Campus
Houston, Texas 77004